Science Technology Engineering Math
STEM STARTERS FOR KIDS

PHYSICS ACTIVITY Book

Packed with activities and physics facts

Written by Jenny Jacoby

Designed and illustrated by Vicky Barker

FOR YOUNG READERS

Racehorse for Young Readers

Racehorse for Young Readers books may be purchased in bulk at special discounts for sales promotions, corporate gifts, fund-raising or education purposes. Special editions can also be created to specifications. For details, contact the Special Sales Department at Skyhorse Publishing, 307 West 36th Street, 11th Floor, New York, NY 10018 or info@skyhorsepublishing.com.

Racehorse for Young Readers is a pending trademark of Skyhorse Publishing, Inc.®, a Delaware corporation.

Visit our website at skyhorsepublishing.com

Printed in China

Copyright © 2018 bsmall publishing ltd.

First Racehorse Publishing Edition 2018

ISBN
978-1-63158-265-3

WHAT IS PHYSICS?

Physics is a way of studying the things in the world around us.
Its name tells us that it is the science of looking at the PHYSICAL
properties of things, studying the way things act because of
things like their shape, size, energy and smoothness.

WHAT IS STEM?

STEM stands for 'science, technology, engineering and mathematics.'
These four areas are closely linked, and physics is an important
part of the science area. When engineers invent things they need to
understand the physics of the materials they use, and they combine
their physics knowledge with math and creative thinking to make
new technologies that make our lives better.

   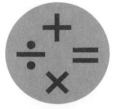

Science   Technology   Engineering   Math

FORCES

Understanding how objects move starts with understanding forces. Forces are pushes and pulls. All around us, forces are acting on everything. Even though objects are sitting still, they are sitting still because the forces are balanced. That means there is the same amount of force pushing an object in one direction as there is pushing it in the opposite direction.

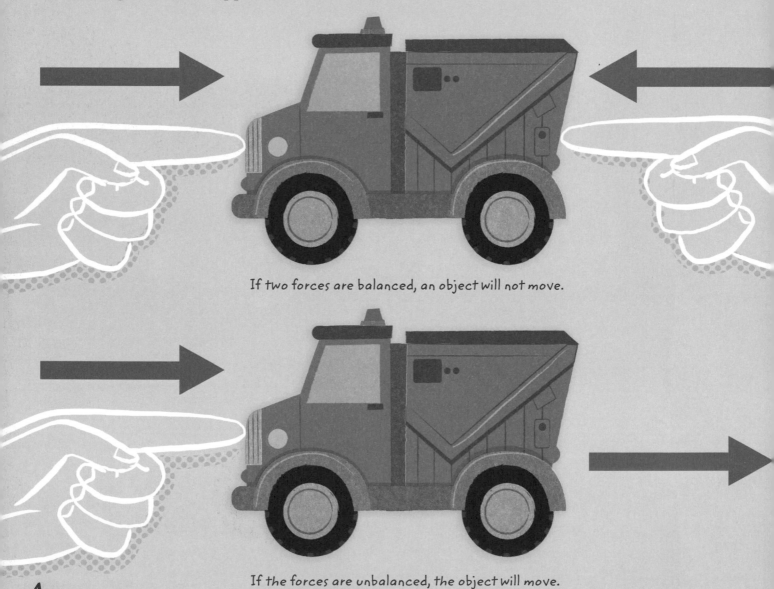

If two forces are balanced, an object will not move.

If the forces are unbalanced, the object will move.

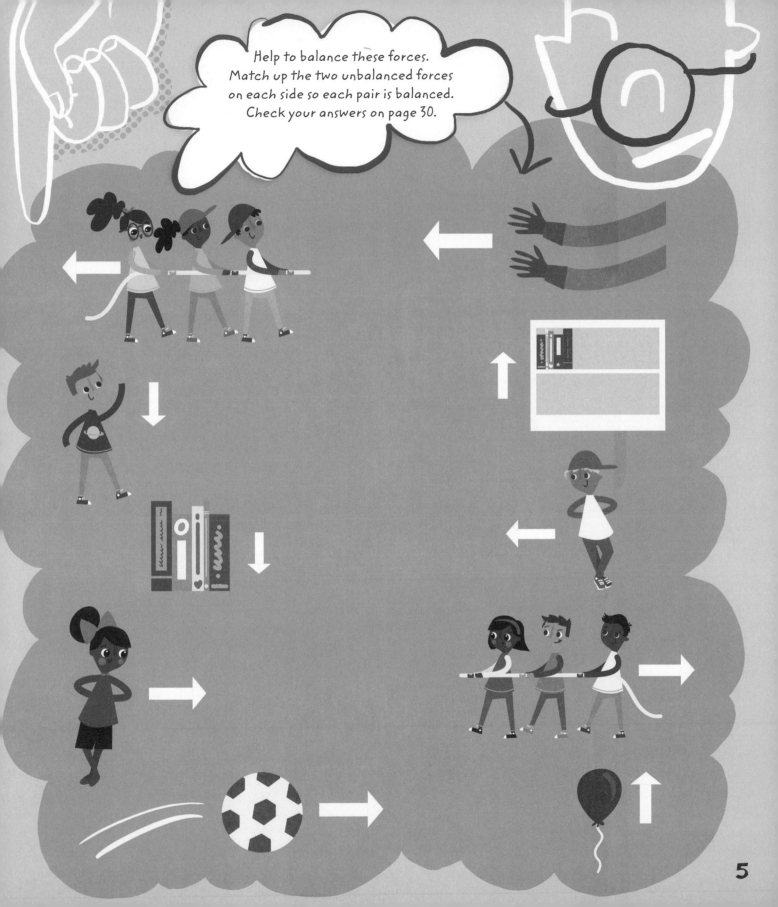

5

GRAVITY

Gravity is an invisible force that pulls things towards the ground. It is why when we jump in the air, we always land back down and don't keep on flying up into the sky.

Gravity is a force that comes from Earth. Each planet has its own force of gravity, and it is different on different planets. The bigger the planet, the bigger the gravity. So on planets smaller than Earth, gravity is less strong. If you visited the moon, which is smaller than Earth, you would feel a lot lighter and be able to jump higher than you can on Earth.

Although gravity has been around since the universe began, it was only discovered about 300 years ago when Sir Isaac Newton noticed an apple falling out of a tree and realized there was a force making that happen.

Sun

Here is a picture of our solar system. Can you put these planets into size order from 1 (the largest) to 8 (the smallest). The largest planet has the strongest gravity, and the smallest planet has the least.

Mercury

Venus

Earth

Mars

Jupiter

Saturn

Uranus

Neptune

If you were in space, where there is very little gravity, you wouldn't be able to sit down unless you were strapped in. You, your hair and clothes would all float! Draw a picture of you floating in space.

ROUGH AND SMOOTH

Friction is a force between two objects that are touching. The force is invisible but, like gravity, we can see its effects. When two objects move against each other, friction can make heat and sound, and slow down movement.

When it's cold, you might rub your hands together for warmth. Friction between your rubbing hands is what causes them to get warm. If you listen closely you will also hear the sound energy given off by your hands.

Some objects cause more friction than others. The smoother an object is, the less friction it produces. Objects designed to travel quickly, like race cars and jet planes, are made of smooth material and built in smooth shapes.

The rougher an object is, the more friction it makes. That makes objects move less easily and resist sliding about. Objects designed to grip and stay put are made of rough material, built in bulky shapes.

Color the items with low resistance in blue, and the items with a lot of resistance in red. Check your answers on page 30.

walking boot

tractor

airplane

sandpaper

submarine

snowshoes

sharp knife

scooter

race car

INERTIA

Look around you and see what the objects are doing. Are they moving about or staying still?

Isaac Newton also discovered the law of inertia: objects stay doing what they are doing, unless a force acts on them. Things don't move by themselves. So, a book will stay sitting on a shelf unless a force moves it – perhaps from a person picking it up. A ball rolling across a football field will keep rolling until the friction of the grass slows it down and stops it.

Search this scene to find each of these objects staying still or moving.

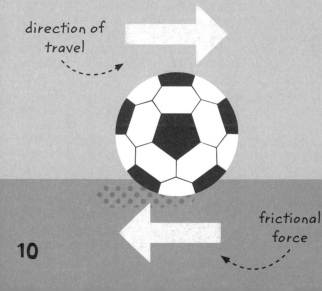

direction of travel

frictional force

- A rock moving because of gravity
- A still rock
- A ball moving because someone has kicked it
- A still apple
- A Frisbee moving because someone has thrown it
- A still Frisbee
- A ball moving because someone has thrown it
- A still ball
- A person moving because of gravity

SPEEDING UP, SLOWING DOWN

An object will only move if a force – like a push, pull or gravity – acts on it. When you kick a ball, your kick is the force, so the ball then accelerates (a big word for 'speeds up') across the ground. The ball goes from standing still to moving fast.

There are two things to know about how objects behave when they accelerate:

1: the heavier an object is the less easy it is to accelerate (a light ball will go faster than a heavy ball)

2: the bigger the force acting on the object (the kick to the ball), the more it will accelerate (the faster the ball will go)

These pair of objects are different weights but the force acting on each one is exactly the same. Color in the one that will speed up more.

12

In these pairs of objects, each one is the same weight but the forces acting on them are different. Color in which object will accelerate the fastest.

EQUAL AND OPPOSITE

Forces always act in pairs. Those pairs are always equal – so they always match in size – and opposite, meaning that a force in one direction is paired with a force in the opposite direction.

When a balloon is blown up but let go of before it's tied, it flies all around the room. This is because the air coming out creates a force going in one direction. Its paired force is equal and opposite, so it sends the balloon flying in the opposite direction with the same force that the air is coming out.

Use your creativity to draw objects, vehicles, people or animals traveling in the opposite direction to the forces shown. Just like the balloon flying through the air.

EVERLASTING ENERGY

Energy is the ability to do work. You use energy to walk up the stairs just as a ball uses energy to roll down a slope. The amazing thing about energy is that it never runs out! It never runs out but it does change form. When it looks like the energy has gone away – when the ball reaches the bottom of the slope it stays still – it hasn't disappeared, just changed.

The ball is full of 'gravitational potential energy,' which means it has the potential to move downwards with the pull of gravity.

Some of the ball's gravitational energy has changed to sound energy and some has changed to movement energy. Some of it still remains as its potential energy for rolling down the slope.

The ball is still again, and all of its gravitational potential energy has changed into other forms of energy.

Help this ball find its way through this maze. Remember, its energy never disappears, just changes from one form to another.

Follow this pattern through the maze as the ball's energy changes from one state to another.

↓ Gravitational potential energy

◉ Movement energy

☼ Sound energy

ELECTRICITY

Electricity is a power that comes from tiny particles called electrons. Electrons are in every material in the world – from your clothes to your food and your hair – but it is when they flow in one direction that they produce electricity.

Electrons have a small charge, and when lots of electrons group together that charge can get large enough to be powerful.

In nature you can see electricity when lightning shoots through the sky. Lightning is a huge number of electrons flowing through the air at once, trying to escape to the earth, and releasing an explosion of light.

Has your hair ever stood on end when you've brushed it, or rubbed a balloon on it? That is electricity too! The hairbrush or balloon passes electrons to your hair, and when so many electrons group together they push each other apart, taking your hair with it.

When we cause the electrons to flow in wires (by using batteries or plugging them into the outlets on the wall) the electricity can be useful. Their power can turn on things we attach to the wire circuits – from lightbulbs to dishwashers.

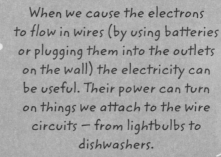

So much of our modern world depends on electricity. Can you spot the seven differences between these two pictures — one with electricity and one without — and imagine your life without electricity? What things are the same?

MAGNETS

A magnet is a piece of rock or metal that can pull certain other metals towards it. Like electricity, magnetism is a natural force that humans have learned to make use of.

Material becomes magnetized when all of its electrons spin in the same direction, and create magnetic field.

A magnet has two opposite ends: a north pole and a south pole. Opposite ends attract, so north poles attract other south poles and repel other north poles.

Magnetic field — the area affected by the magnet

N

S

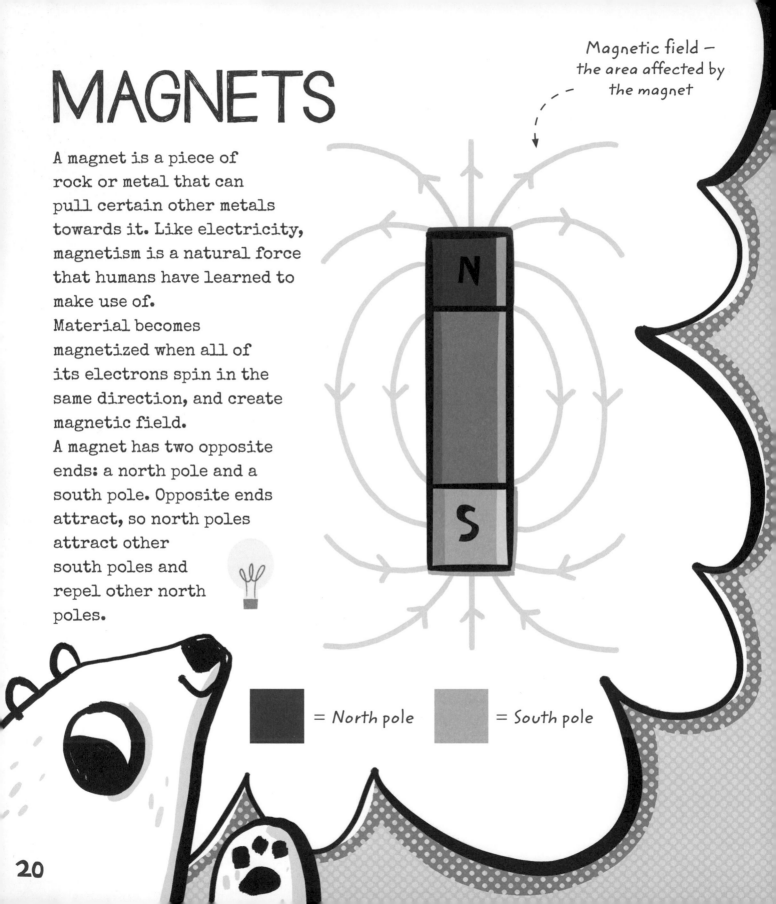

■ = North pole   ■ = South pole

21

THE BIG BANG

Physicists believe that the universe was created about 14 billion years ago, when the 'big bang' happened. It was a giant explosion that turned energy into matter, and over a very long time that matter developed into our universe, including our galaxy, our solar system, and Earth as we know it.

One reason people believe in the big bang theory is because physics tells us how much of certain chemical elements exist in the universe, and that quantity matches what we think was created in the big bang.

The **UNIVERSE** is made up of more stars than we can count, in billions of galaxies.

A **GALAXY** is a collection of millions or billions of stars, held together by gravity.

MATTER is a word physicists use for anything that takes up space — from atoms to rocks and people.

Physicists estimate how much helium was created in the big bang. The same amount of helium was present at the big bang as is around in the universe now. Helium is an atom, which is made up of two protons (the red balls) and two neutrons (the grey balls).

Can you find 15 helium atoms in this big bang picture, and 15 helium atoms in the picture of the present?

BIG BANG

PRESENT

SPACE

Planet Earth is one of eight planets in our solar system. All of the planets are spinning: they spin around themselves and they orbit around the sun. The Earth spins around at 1000 miles per hour. The moon orbits around the Earth and the Earth orbits the sun.

A planet is an object in space that orbits around a star. The sun is the Earth's star.

Orbit means to travel around an object.

IT TAKES...

1 day

for the Earth to spin around once. It's daytime for us when our side of the Earth faces the sun, and night-time when our side of the Earth faces away.

Night

Day

1 month

for the moon to orbit the Earth.

1 year

for the Earth to orbit the sun.

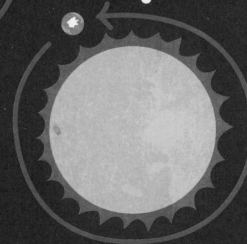

Can you find these spacey words in this wordsearch?
They can be up, down, sideways, diagonal or backwards.

```
b h t r a e l d j x y d p o h v p
y o j u p i t e r i l q g x o r l
m o c y i l x v u e l p y z n t a
b e s k o k l g c b a k r x e e n
h a j o r b i t o d a a d s p u e
l n l i t i u n k c t h l i t b t
k f z y j l t t j s v e t l u b a
h y m o o n u r c t u p l m n u i
e c v x t g j e n g i n p a e d l
v r s u i o p o n l o v u k m o p
d e t u m c u i o r l r u f d e l
c y n p a k e n k y u d r x y t m
s t j u r b c p z t i t n o k l o
d s y i s y f d t z h p a m j u o
e y v n u s k u j a m p o s e y m
f u s e l a g e v n i t c r i y j
m e r c u r y s e o j n v t h x k
```

earth   moon   sun

jupiter   neptune   venus

mars   planet   orbit

mercury   saturn   star

25

SPEED OF SOUND

Sound travels in 'waves.' A thing making a sound vibrates. Those vibrations make sound waves, which travel in all directions through the air, liquids and solids. To hear a sound, you need an ear, which can turn sound waves into messages to your brain about what you're hearing.

The guitar string vibrates.

Sound waves travel through the air.

An ear picks up the sound wave.

Sound waves travel at different speeds depending on what they're traveling through. On a warm day, sound travels through air at 344 metres per second. On a hot day, sound travels faster. But sound travels faster still through liquids, like water, and some solids, like rock and metal. Other materials, like foam, are bad at transmitting sound waves and people use them to 'sound proof' or catch sound waves and stop them from traveling on.

Which of these materials are good for transmitting sound waves? Circle them in red.

Which of these materials are good for sound-proofing? Circle them in blue.

27

LIGHT

Light travels much, much faster than sound. In just one second, light can travel all the way to the moon. In that time, sound has only traveled the length of three football pitches. That's why in a storm you often see lightning a few seconds before you hear the thunder, even though the two start at exactly the same moment.

Light cannot travel around a corner. Light bounces off objects and we see objects because of the light that bounces off them. That is why we can't see things in the dark, and why we can't see things around corners.

One way to see around a corner is using a mirror. Because the mirror is a shiny, reflective surface, the light bounces off it in another direction.

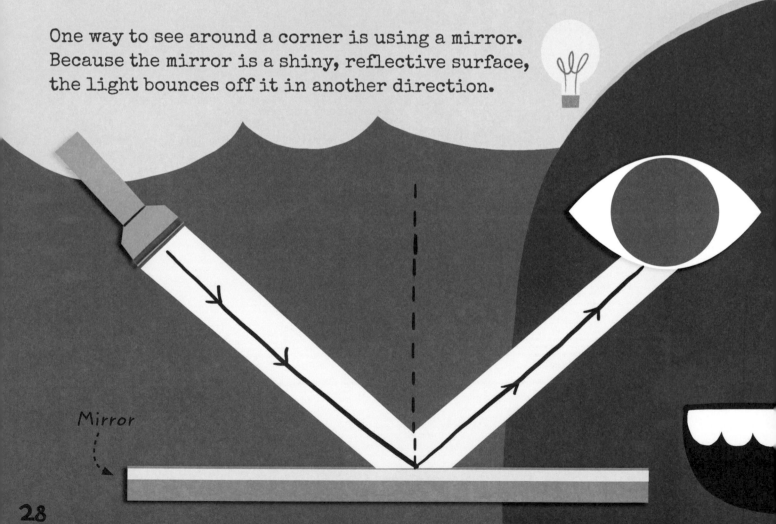

Mirror

Help the light find its way through this maze. Remember, it can only travel around a corner when a mirror is there to help it. Look for this symbol at corners to help the light move around the corner:

FINISH

START

ANSWERS

page 4-5

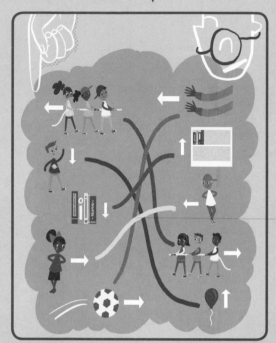

page 8-9

page 6-7

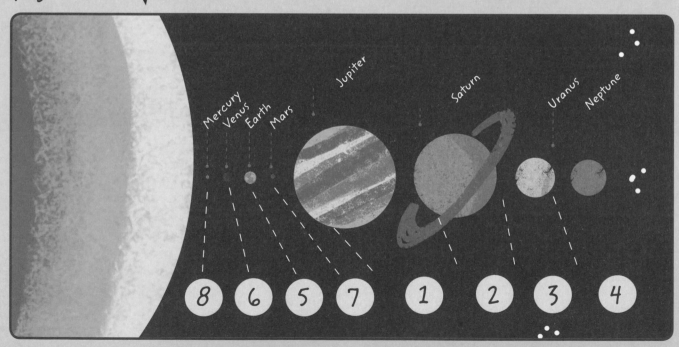

Mercury Venus Earth Mars Jupiter Saturn Uranus Neptune

8 6 5 7 1 2 3 4

page 10-11

page 12-13

page 16-17

page 18-19

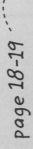

page 20-21

page 22-23

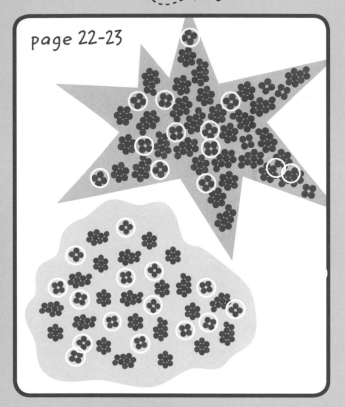

page 24-25

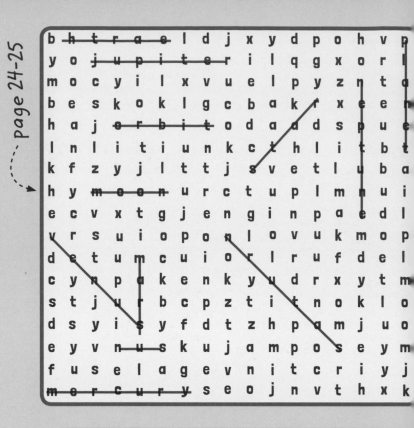

b	h	t	r	a	e	l	d	j	x	y	d	p	o	h	v	p
y	o	j	u	p	i	t	e	r	i	l	q	g	x	o	r	l
m	o	c	y	i	l	x	v	u	e	l	p	y	z	n	t	a
b	e	s	k	o	k	l	g	c	b	a	k	r	x	e	e	n
h	a	j	e	r	b	i	t	o	d	a	d	d	s	p	u	e
l	n	l	i	t	i	u	n	k	c	t	h	l	i	t	b	t
k	f	z	y	j	l	t	t	j	s	v	e	t	l	u	b	a
h	y	m	o	o	n	u	r	c	t	u	p	l	m	n	u	i
e	c	v	x	t	g	j	e	n	g	i	n	p	a	e	d	l
v	r	s	u	i	o	p	o	n	l	o	v	u	k	m	o	p
d	e	t	u	m	c	u	i	o	r	l	r	u	f	d	e	l
c	y	n	p	a	k	e	n	k	y	u	d	r	x	y	t	m
s	t	j	u	r	b	c	p	z	t	i	t	n	o	k	l	o
d	s	y	i	s	y	f	d	t	z	h	p	a	m	j	u	o
e	y	v	n	u	s	k	u	j	a	m	p	o	s	e	y	m
f	u	s	e	l	a	g	e	v	n	i	t	c	r	i	y	j
m	e	r	c	u	r	y	s	e	o	j	n	v	t	h	x	k

page 26-27

page 28-29